Community Helpers

Helping in the Community

by Trudy Becker

www.focusreaders.com

Copyright © 2024 by Focus Readers®, Mendota Heights, MN 55120. All rights reserved. No part of this book may be reproduced or utilized in any form or by any means without written permission from the publisher.

Focus Readers is distributed by North Star Editions:
sales@northstareditions.com | 888-417-0195

Produced for Focus Readers by Red Line Editorial.

Photographs ©: Shutterstock Images, cover, 1, 15, 17; iStockphoto, 4, 7, 8, 11, 12, 18, 21

Library of Congress Cataloging-in-Publication Data
Library of Congress Cataloging-in-Publication Data is available on the Library of Congress website.

ISBN
979-8-88998-017-9 (hardcover)
979-8-88998-060-5 (paperback)
979-8-88998-144-2 (ebook pdf)
979-8-88998-103-9 (hosted ebook)

Printed in the United States of America
Mankato, MN
012024

About the Author

Trudy Becker lives in Minneapolis, Minnesota. She likes exploring new places and loves anything involving books.

Table of Contents

CHAPTER 1
A Helping Hand 5

CHAPTER 2
Helping the Elderly 9

CHAPTER 3
Helping Make Rules 13

THAT'S AMAZING!
Helping Nature 16

CHAPTER 4
Local Groups 19

Focus on Helping in the Community • 22
Glossary • 23
To Learn More • 24
Index • 24

Chapter 1

A Helping Hand

A boy and his mom walk to the hospital. They aren't going to see a doctor. They are **volunteers**. They bring cards and flowers. They have games, too.

In the hospital, they spend time with patients. Other helpers clean up. Some sort **supplies**. When they are done, the helpers feel good. They helped their **community**.

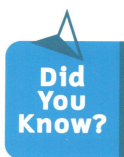

Did You Know? People don't need to be doctors to help at hospitals.

Chapter 2

Helping the Elderly

Elderly people live in many communities. They might need extra help. Volunteers can help them with chores. They can mow lawns. They can fix broken things.

Some elderly people live in **nursing homes**. They get lots of help there. But they might be lonely. So, volunteers can visit. They can talk to the people who live there. Having company helps them feel better.

Did You Know? Younger people need extra care, too. Helpers might babysit young people.

Chapter 3

Helping Make Rules

Communities have many rules. **Governments** make those rules. They might decide where a road can be built. Or they might decide how a town spends its money.

Town governments have meetings. They talk about the rules. Other people can go to the meetings. They can share their ideas. That can help the town get better.

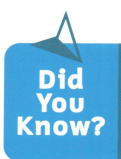
Did You Know? Even young people can share thoughts at town meetings.

THAT'S AMAZING!

Helping Nature

Protecting nature is a great way to help the community. Some helpers plant trees. Others pick up trash. And some teach people about **recycling**. Recycling helps less trash end up in nature.

Chapter 4

Local Groups

Supporting **local** groups helps the community, too. Many communities have music or dance groups. Helpers can find places for groups to perform. And they can go to shows.

Some towns might have art groups. Volunteers can give them supplies. People use the supplies to draw, paint, and more. They can make the towns beautiful.

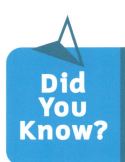

Did You Know? Art and music can help bring people together.

FOCUS ON
Helping in the Community

Write your answers on a separate piece of paper.

1. Write a sentence that explains how volunteers could help elderly people in the community.
2. Which way of helping the community do you think is most useful? Why?
3. Who makes rules for a community?
   - A. the hospital
   - B. the government
   - C. the volunteers
4. How could sharing ideas at meetings help governments make better rules?
   - A. Governments could hear more ideas.
   - B. Governments could forget ideas.
   - C. Governments have no ideas.

Answer key on page 24.

Glossary

community
A group of people and the places where they spend time.

elderly
Old. Usually over the age of 65.

governments
The people and groups that run cities, states, tribes, or countries.

local
Having to do with a nearby area.

nursing homes
Places where some elderly people live and get taken care of.

protecting
Keeping something safe.

recycling
Using an old item to make something new.

supplies
Items that people need to do something.

volunteers
People who help without being paid.

To Learn More

BOOKS

Rebman, Nick. *Reduce, Reuse, Recycle*. Lake Elmo, MN: Focus Readers, 2022.

Ventura, Marne. *Government and Community*. Minneapolis: Abdo Publishing, 2019.

NOTE TO EDUCATORS

Visit **www.focusreaders.com** to find lesson plans, activities, links, and other resources related to this title.

Index

E
elderly, 9–10

H
hospital, 5–6

N
nature, 16

T
town meetings, 14

Answer Key: 1. Answers will vary; 2. Answers will vary; 3. B; 4. A